·MY · FIRST · LOOK · AT ·
Numbers

A DORLING KINDERSLEY BOOK

Note to Parents

My First Look at Numbers is designed to help young children develop their counting skills. It's a book for you and your child to share and enjoy – looking at the pages together, finding and counting familiar objects, learning to recognize and name numbers, and using new words.

Have fun with numbers!

Senior Editor Jane Yorke
Art Editor Toni Rann
Photography Stephen Oliver
Series Consultant Neil Morris
Editorial Director Sue Unstead
Art Director Anne-Marie Bulat

Published in Great Britain
by Dorling Kindersley Limited,
9 Henrietta Street, London WC2E 8PS

Paperback edition
2 4 6 8 10 9 7 5 3 1

Visit us on the World Wide Web at
http://www.dk.com

A CIP catalogue record for this book is available from the British Library.

ISBN 0 7513 6622 6

Phototypeset by Windsorgraphics, Ringwood, Hampshire
Reproduced in Hong Kong by Bright Arts
Printed and bound in Singapore by Imago

· MY · FIRST · LOOK · AT
Numbers

DK

DORLING KINDERSLEY
London • New York • Moscow • Sydney

1

one teddy bear

2

two shoes

3

three
flowers

4

four
butterflies

5

five cakes

6

six hats

7
seven
shells

8

eight
brushes

9
nine
gloves

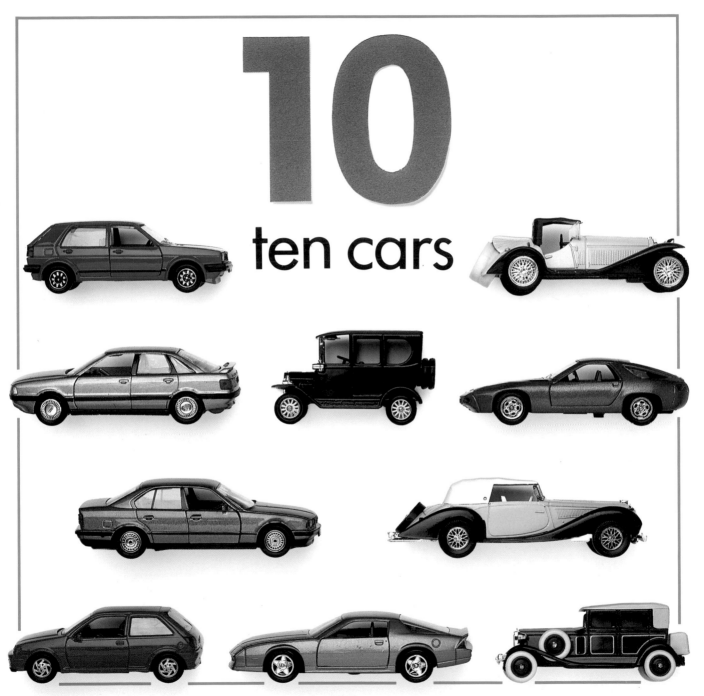

10
ten cars

20

twenty
crayons

100

one hundred sweets

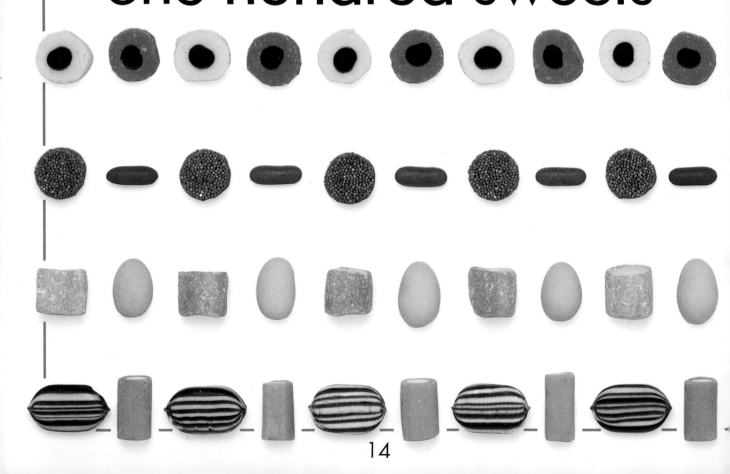

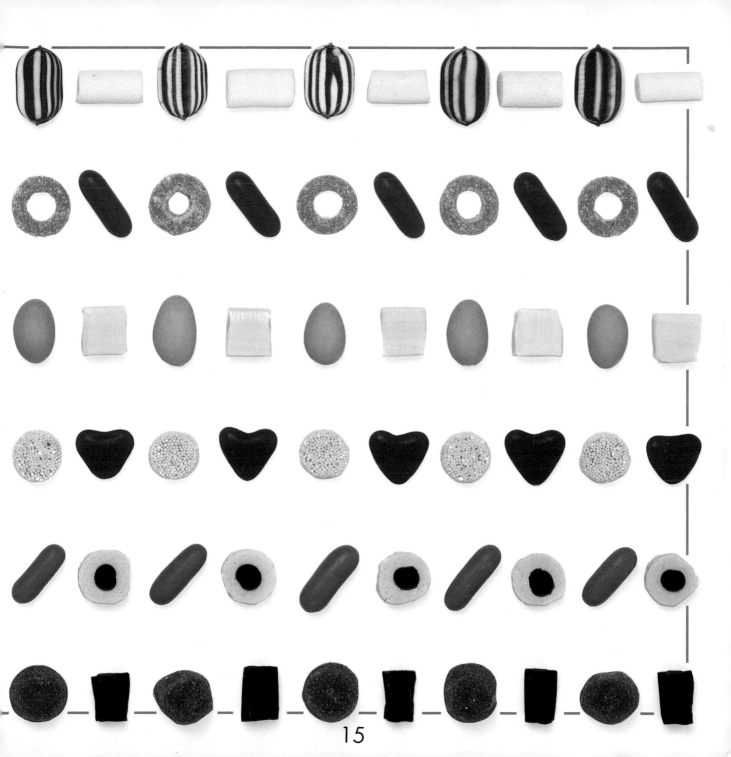

How many?

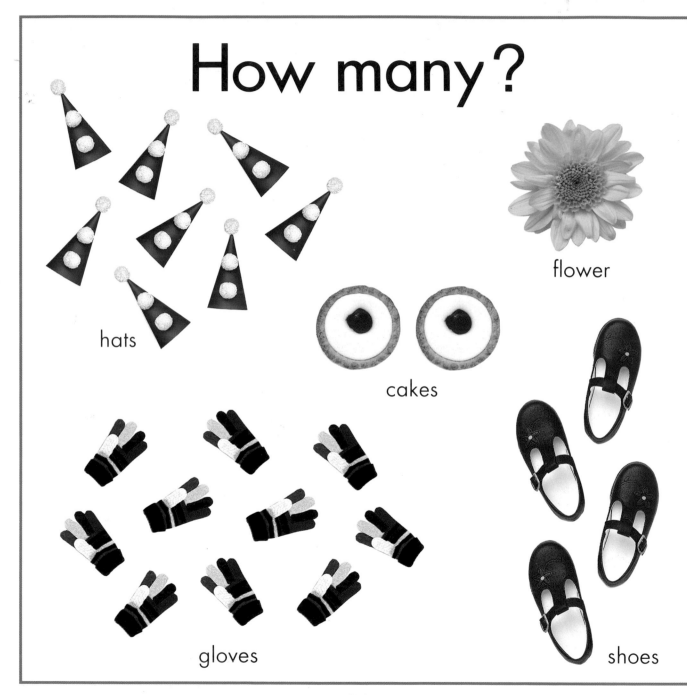

hats

flower

cakes

gloves

shoes

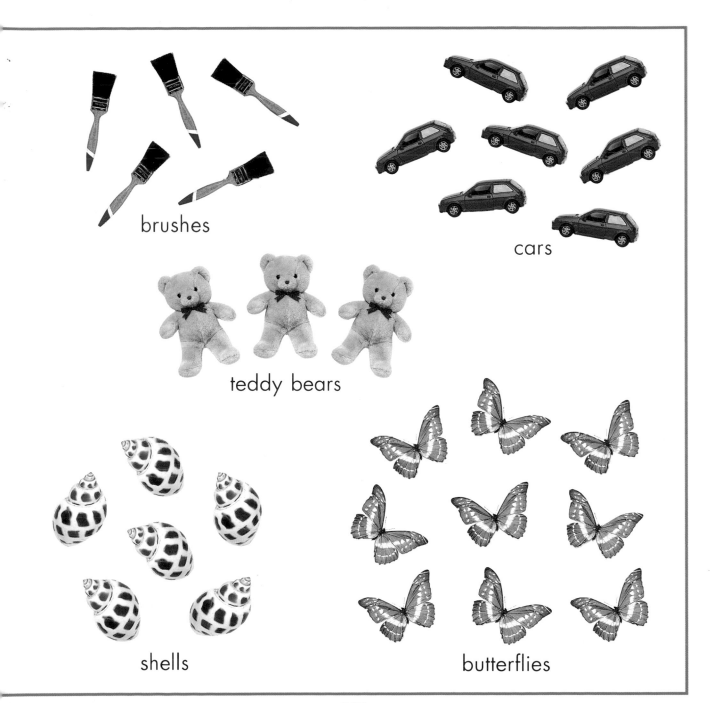

brushes

cars

teddy bears

shells

butterflies